It's Raining Candidates

Easy techniques and strategies to get great results from
your recruitment suppliers in a candidate-short market.

Simon Berry

It's Raining Candidates
Simon Berry

ISBN 978-1-914615-69-6

A CIP catalogue record for this book is available from the British Library.

Published 2023
Tricorn Books, Treadgolds
Bishop Street
Portsmouth PO1 3HN
www.tricornbooks.co.uk

It's Raining Candidates

Easy techniques and strategies to get great results from your recruitment suppliers in a candidate-short market.

Contents

Foreword

Neil Carberry

Chief Executive of the Recruitment
& Employment Confederation (REC)

From technology to demography, the jobs market is in a state of high-speed change. Employers are currently navigating the retirement of the sizeable "baby boom" generation at the same time as the end of free movement, the results of a pandemic and a huge change in skills needs. For many business leaders, these big economic trends can seem overwhelming, but there are changes that every business can make to become more effective at sourcing and keeping the best people.

This especially includes how you select, interact, and engage with your recruitment suppliers. Taking your professional relationship from that of a one-off transaction to a deeper delivery 'partnership' based on a design that suits your business; this is a far more effective approach to tackling the current talent shortage challenges.

Simon Berry has written a 'handbook' to help you successfully achieve this. An excellent guide for any SME, this book will help you find the recruitment partner and arrangement that is right for you, giving you a much-improved chance of building the workforce you need.

Prequel and introduction

Who's this book for?

This book is <u>not</u> another book on how to recruit. This book is not for job seekers either. This book is for people in business that have used recruitment services in the past, or plan to use them in the future, to help them find the people they need to grow their business. This book is for business owners, HR professionals, department managers, hiring managers and anyone that needs to engage with a recruiter, either for the first time or for the 1,000th time, to help them find and employ the people they need.

This book is especially for anyone who has found working with a recruiter to be frustrating, disappointing, or less efficient or fruitful than had been hoped.

This book is also for anyone who receives unwanted (and sometimes overwhelming) enquiries and sales calls from recruiters. This book will help you protect yourself and your existing team from the time burden of dealing with these.

In this book you will find ideas, techniques, strategies and insight that will massively improve the results you get from recruiters, if you choose to employ them.

Recruiters… While this book isn't aimed at you specifically, I do believe this will be a very useful read for existing recruiters. As a recruiter, if you can understand these ideas and techniques then you are in a position to better explain them to your clients. It will be different to anything you have read before, giving you a different angle on your profession. When writing this book, I often think back to the film Jerry Maguire and the scene where Tom Cruise is desperately pleading with his key client. "Help me help you!", he kept repeating. If you are a recruiter reading this book, you will be much better prepared to 'help your clients help you' and further your working relationship to one of a true partnership, benefitting you both much more. Who knows... you might even decide to give all new clients a copy of this book to help them find the best ways to work with you.

My aim for this book
I have been involved in recruitment for my entire working career. I've owned and run recruitment businesses, acted as a consultant for other business owners and I've used recruitment services, both as a job seeker many years ago and as a B2B client. Throughout that time, I've been very aware of the many misunderstandings and false beliefs about how most of these businesses work.

Many businesses get frustrated with the quality of service or results that they get from recruiters. Of course, sometimes this is because that particular recruitment business is no good. Fundamentally though, I believe that this frustration is usually down to false beliefs and misunderstandings. With these removed, working relationships can improve and successful partnerships can develop quickly. We all know that having access to great people can have an immeasurably positive impact on your business.

When talking with a family friend a few years ago, I had a blinding flash of the obvious. My friend was a successful business owner and someone I respect very much. He was talking about how frustrated he was with recruiters.

"They charge really high fees. I've managed to negotiate them right down but it is still far too high for what they do. And none of them are getting me any results. They constantly keep pestering me for information. And when they do finally send someone through, they aren't at all right." He was clearly frustrated with his recruitment suppliers, but when we broke it down it was clear why he wasn't getting results.

Firstly, I posed the question to him: How much time did you invest when initially engaging with your suppliers, to ensure that they understood what you are looking for? Were you confident that they had the information they needed to proactively promote you as the ideal next employer? It quickly became apparent that my friend was expecting them to know things, when actually they had no idea. As Michael Bungay Stanier said in his book (The Coaching Habit), "the problem with communication is the illusion that it has taken place". That then explained why they were chasing him for more information all the time. My friend was asking them to recruit blind, and it had never really occurred to him before, at least not to that degree.

We then looked into his understanding of what a recruiter actually does. We were both quite surprised at how far off his understanding was. With a new appreciation of the volume of work and the skills involved in the role, this then threw a whole new spotlight onto his perception of what the fees should be. We established that the people he was seeking were in low supply and high demand, and that the recruiters he was working with would likely have more than one client looking for that particular skill set. It was little surprise then that, having negotiated the fees so low, he was no longer their priority.

11

Following that conversation, my friend decided to visit two of his recruitment suppliers, invest time in them to help them understand his business, so that they were much better equipped to actually 'sell' it as a potential employer of choice. He also renegotiated the fee, not massively, but so that both parties were still happy. My friend told me that this had a huge effect on the results he received.

Since then, my friend has told me that he regularly and proactively calls his recruiters to tell them about new things going on in the business and finds opportunities to keep him and his business in the front of their minds. He is now taking total responsibility to do everything he can to help them get great results for him.

I believe that a strong understanding of how a recruiter works is an empowering position for any hirer to get the best results out of a recruiter and at the best value possible. By writing this book, my aim is to markedly improve the recruitment sector; for the sector itself, and for those that are business customers of the industry. I will do this by creating empathy and understanding from those who have never worked in recruitment but do need the help of a recruiter to further their own businesses. If people have a better understanding, they will have appropriately high levels of expectations, and this will in turn help weed out the people and businesses that operate in our sector but who don't conduct themselves professionally.

I also believe that, if recruiters and end hirers are working more harmoniously together, then they will have much less reason to be frustrated with each other, increasing positivity in the industry significantly.

It's a big goal and the only way I can achieve this is if lots of people read this book. So, to help me achieve this I would be grateful if you could review it on Amazon once you've read it!

Thank you for reading this book. I don't claim to be a skilled writer and have written it as I would have spoken it. Even so, I am confident that it will be a very useful investment of your time.

Simon Berry
Author

How to get the best out of recruitment consultancies – a consultant's perspective

The purpose of this book is not to offer an analysis of the recruitment industry, but to provide an invaluable insider's view of how things really work in a recruitment company and provide real world, proactive ideas for how you and your business can ensure that you get what you want from the recruitment industry. After all, your employees are what makes your business.

The recruitment industry is incredibly diverse and is filled with many brilliant people and businesses. It also has its share of cowboys and corner cutters. It is no secret that the recruitment industry has struggled with a poor reputation on occasions. Many companies and hiring managers have had bad experiences using agencies in the past and are reluctant to use one again. Other companies will be open to the concept but will not get the service they require, perhaps receiving a handful of semi-relevant CVs before being left high and dry, despite being promised so much to begin with. Of course, there are also some extremely effective and professional companies out there too.

However, finding the right suppliers and working well with them can have a profoundly positive impact on your business.

This book will help you navigate through to the best the industry has to offer and give you the tools to extract outstanding results from those companies.

'What can you do to help the agency?'

It is a strange thought initially. You should reasonably be able to expect a recruitment agency to tell you what it can and can't do and then proceed to offer you the service you require. Why should you have to give thought to what you can do to help? 'Surely that is their job' you would have thought! It might not be your natural approach to stand back and think... 'OK, how am I going to help this company help me?' But if you do take this approach, if you invest an hour or two to read this book, you will find yourself grumbling a lot less about recruitment companies and find that there is a great deal more to be gained from them than you originally thought.

If men are from Mars and women are from Venus, where the heck are recruiters from?

Why am I asking this question? I believe it is important that a customer of a recruitment firm has a basic working understanding of the challenges the recruiter is faced with, such that the two parties can work together more efficiently and help each other out wherever possible for the benefit of all involved.

Let's have a closer look into what makes a good recruiter and what makes them tick.

The recruitment industry used to be well-known for huge profits and sleazy, pushy sales types. Generally though, this was a stereotype as opposed to the truth, for the vast majority at least.

Since then, the industry has become hugely competitive, and it has had to reinvent itself several times over to remain current and lean enough to remain profitable. It's a tough industry. There are currently in the region of 30,000 recruitment agencies in the UK alone, providing employment to just over 200,000 people. In 2021, around 6,000 recruitment and staffing companies were registered at Companies House (UK). However, despite the huge volume of new businesses each year, the total isn't growing all that much. Almost as many businesses are folding each year.

It's a tough sector and only good businesses stand the test of time: ones that offer a strong customer experience and that are efficient at fulfilling their purpose.

It's no easier a ride for the individuals within the business. Staff turnover has always been high in the sector. *The Times* newspaper once produced an article stating that the job of a recruitment consultant is the number one most stressful office job in the world. While I find this hard to believe, it nevertheless raises the point that it definitely is not an easy job.

Good recruiters have a varied job to do. We're not proposing that they are in the same bracket as rocket scientists. But they do need an incredibly diverse set of skills.

First, they need to have a very strong work ethic. Client and candidates do not come easily. They will also need thick skin and a significant amount of resilience to be able to cope with all the rejection.

They need to be great at relationship-building and generating trust and rapport. They are looking to have conversations with hundreds of candidates about things that are very personal to them and this takes some fairly advanced people skills to be able to do well. It's also a vitally important part of the role. As a client, you will want to know that your recruiter has accessed the root of the reasons as to why he or she is looking to leave their current employer, or why your own firm is the right choice for that individual, such that you can trust that they will stay with you for the long term.

A modern recruiter also needs to be great at written work and producing content that attracts the right people to your company. They need to be skilled in the inner workings of social media and modern marketing techniques, which is vital for there to be any chance of attracting enough good candidates to achieve strong results for clients.

Recruiters are salespeople

The role of a recruiter is a sales role. Every element of the role involves sales to some extent, at least. The biggest challenge is that the product being sold is a human. And unfortunately, there is no shelf in the warehouse full of skilled humans.

So, the sales process looks roughly like this:

1. Sell recruitment service offering to a client.
2. Sell recruitment service offering and/or client's employment offering to the candidate. The candidate is usually hard to find, hard to contact, highly desirable by multiple organisations and well-protected and valued by their existing employer.
3. Sell the candidate to the client (Introduction stage).
4. IF the client and the candidate like each other, sell the package offering to the candidate in an effort to close the deal.

There is so much that can go wrong in this process and if any single thing does go wrong the whole process fails. Imagine a scenario where a car salesman shows a customer the perfect car. The customer loves the car and agrees to buy the car at the asking price. Then the car turns around and says, "Well that's all very flattering, however this just isn't the new owner for me." A recruiter's 'product' is a human being and has a mind of his or her own. This naturally throws a few unexpected curve balls into the process.

A good recruiter should be well-positioned to minimise these by gaining the trust of the candidate and having a strong working knowledge of what his or her true motivations and agendas are. Yet there will always be some disappointments along the way.

Are recruiters too money motivated?

Yes... Recruiters are generally motivated by money. Nevertheless, the good ones also care about customer experience and really get a kick out of helping people with something that is of real importance to them. Again, this is a strong trait of the best recruiters. They will understand that career choices are some of the most stressful but significant, exciting and important life decisions that people have to make. They hold the belief that people should have the right support and advice to help them make the best choices possible along the way, while doing their best to make the process fun and enjoyable.

So now we've covered what a recruiter is and does, let's look at how you can work with them to get great results from them, for your own hiring needs.

Negotiation techniques and concepts

Let's dive straight into the subject that most people want to see efficiencies in more than anything…

Fees
Ever since recruitment companies were invented, businesses have been renegotiating placement fees and contractor percentages. This will always be the case because cost and profit management is vital to any business. That means, however, that percentage fees are also vital to the recruitment business.

Often, the first thing a business will do when speaking to a recruitment agency is attempt to agree the lowest fees possible. The important but simple point here is this: if you negotiate too low, initially you will assume that you have a good deal. The reality is that the agency will put your requirements right at the bottom of its priority list. The recruitment industry is a ruthlessly competitive industry and gone are the days where agencies are generating huge amounts of money regardless of their ability. Due to competition, margins in recruitment are tight these days. These are commercial organisations and they have to work very hard indeed to make a profit. As an example, it might be that a consultant will have a choice of working on your vacancy offering 10% for a perm placement, or your opposition's vacancy offering 20%. It is likely that that the consultant will send the good CVs to the other company and the poorer ones to you. At worst, they may not look at your vacancy at all.

Of course, I am not saying that fee negotiation is to be avoided. I believe all agencies are open to fee negotiation.

But a measure of caution is highly advisable, otherwise you will be getting nothing but false economy. This is a common reason why many businesses experience a poor service from agencies. The important thing is to not price yourself into receiving a poor service from all the agencies with whom you do business. Ultimately, the key to successful negotiation is finding the point where both parties are happy. If either side is less than happy about the agreement, something is bound to go wrong somewhere along the line.

Be very wary of agencies that come to the table offering very low rates. If they don't value themselves then there is very little chance that you will get the level of service and results that your business requires and deserves.

Different industries, skill sets and skill levels will command different average percentage rates. Before negotiating fees, do your best to find out what similar companies have agreed, effectively benchmarking the industry. Perhaps your suppliers or customers will have some input for you on this. If you have already agreed fees with an agency but are unsatisfied with the service you are receiving, ask them what more they can do for you if you increase the fee. After all, in the majority of cases it will be a 'no placement, no fee' scenario.

Finally, be aware that you may benefit from changing the fee for different scenarios and vacancy types or urgencies, even on a one-off basis. Regardless of the overriding agreement that you have in place with a supplier, there may be some strong advantages to making exceptions to this, with mutual agreement.

For example, you may find yourself in a situation where you have a different kind of vacancy which you believe to be easier to fill. Don't be afraid to float the idea with them and explain that you would like some help, but that you can't justify the usual fee for this particular hire. The worst that they can say is no.

Plus, if you have a vacancy that is a critical hire, could it be worth speaking with your supplier and offering an increased fee or incentive? I've seen this work very effectively for clients many times over. A recent example was a large national nursing home business. They have hundreds of nursing homes across the UK and around 300 live nursing roles at any one time. They had one critical home which was struggling with recruitment, to the extent that they were faced with having to shut the home down if they couldn't turn this around quickly. They chose to double their recruitment fee payable, just for that one home, in an effort to incentivise their suppliers.

There were two key benefits to this. The recruiters were money-motivated and were excited about working on these vacancies in the hope of securing a higher fee. Secondly, they were equally as motivated by the fact that they now understood just how important this was to their client. Both had the effect that this vacancy was not only prioritised, but the consultants went 'all in' to assist the client, taking actions and initiatives that were well above and beyond the normal processes.

The hiring business was extremely pleased with the response they received as a result of increasing the fee on a one-off basis, and they filled the roles much quicker than they could have ever realistically expected.

Other aspects of the terms

Of course, there is a lot more to business terms and conditions than just the fee, but the same principles apply to all. You as a business want to receive the best value possible. The terms you sign up to are only one aspect of this value, but they are an important part. Don't be afraid of looking into what is negotiable. Again though, don't take it too far or you will lose the motivation of the agency to find you the right people and offer you their best service. If you are concerned by a particularly short rebate period or an unusually tight payment date, then question it, but stick to what is reasonable. Perhaps base it on the terms of another recruitment service provider.

Something for something

If you are looking to negotiate on an aspect of your working relationship, consider what you are willing to offer in return. For example, if your concern is over the fee, perhaps you could propose that they lower their fee in return for a period of exclusivity to work on your role, or to pay on short payment terms, if your cashflow position allows for it. This way, you might be keeping their interest and motivation at the same time as getting a better deal.

Agency fees might appear unreasonably expensive, but unless you have worked for an agency before, you would likely be surprised by just how much work (and cost) goes into the recruitment process. A good consultant will often invest several days of work into one vacancy, making hundreds of calls in the process, advertising the role, and promoting it through various social media channels. They will also be applying their skills as a good communicator and networker to find you the right candidates. Finally, you're tapping into their network, talent community and/ or database, which has the potential to yield that ideal but elusive candidate. That network has taken years of invested time, advertising budget and skill to build in the first place. In today's world, skilled candidates are increasingly in short supply in most industries, and recruiters are having to go further, and spend more, to find that talent. It is often an intensive and expensive process.

As a side note, be wary of agencies that come straight to the table with unusually favourable terms. This is often due to them having to compete on price because they are an underperforming company. As with anything, you invariably get what you pay for.

The rebate period

All professional recruiters should offer a rebate period. These vary hugely across different sectors but regardless, there should be a clause which stipulates that, should someone leave their employment early on, there is a refund of some sort. This should be the case regardless of whether it was the client or the candidate that made the choice to bring the employment to an end.

A rebate structure will usually start at 100% and reduces over time. An example might look like this:

Week of employment in which candidate leaves	% of introduction fee refunded
Week 1–2	100%
Week 3–4	75%
Week 5–6	50%
Week 7–8	10%

This represents an eight-week period which is probably the minimum you should expect. It is normal for some sectors to have much longer rebate periods.

You will notice that the rebate percentage reduces over time, and this leads us to a top tip: **If, in the first few days, you get the feeling that you may have hired the wrong person, you need to act quickly and decisively**. You need to be fair to the candidate who has shown interest and faith in your organisation, but you also need to be mindful of your rebate structure.

If you have concerns, the first thing I would recommend is to speak to your recruiter. It may be that they would be willing to extend the rebate period, rather than forcing you into a quick decision that could well result in them having to give you back the full amount. You would then have more time and less pressure to evaluate the individual's suitability for your role or business.

If your concerns are regarding whether the candidate is committed, as opposed to regarding their ability, your recruiter may be able to get you some answers here. Often a new hire will confide in their recruiter more than they will the new hirer. Depending on your relationship with that recruiter, it may be that they can influence things to your advantage. To be clear, I'm not advocating that they release information about a conversation that happened in confidence. Often, a recruiter can uncover the reason that person isn't fully committed. That consultant may then be able to encourage them to speak with their employer. Alternatively, they may be able to get their consent, so the recruiter is free to brief you. With knowledge of the issue, it can often be repaired. It's surprising how often it is something small and fixable that could easily be put right with the proper clarity and communication.

Recruiters tend to feel very strongly about rebate periods and, once agreed, will rarely budge on them if the issue isn't raised in advance. Requesting an improved rebate only after someone has left is likely to fall on deaf ears. This is because the recruiter will have done no less work as a result of the person leaving. Often the truth is that that person left due to a failure of the new employer to deliver on the promises made at interview. But if you have that conversation with your recruiter in advance, and explain the issue, your chances are much improved.

Never negotiate in hindsight

The vast majority of recruiting businesses or hiring managers would never dream of doing this. So, my apologies if this would never apply to you. I'm including this in the book at the request of a few recruiters who have been affected by it. I think that, when understood by a hiring manager, it will ultimately lead to a better working relationship and help avoid significant pitfalls.

For contingent recruitment, a recruiter has to do a huge amount of work with zero guarantee of actually getting paid for it. Contingent recruitment means that there are no fees up front, or at any point until you successfully hire someone. If for any reason the hiring company changes their mind, decides not to hire, or changes their criteria slightly, all that work is wasted and there is no comeback for the recruiter. Recruiters are also often pitted against each other in competition, under the contingency model. This is another obvious reminder to the recruiter that they have no guarantee of getting paid for the work that they are doing. Very few other industries ever do this. That's all well and fine. Recruiters have learnt to be at peace with this. They know the risk, but they also know the upside if they do their job well and make a placement.

By negotiating in hindsight, I'm referring to a deliberate attempt to alter the fee that the recruiter thought was already pre-agreed and signed off. It is a sure-fire way to damage a working relationship with a contingent recruiter. If you try to renegotiate a fee at the point of offer, or at any time other than before instructing them with a role, you'll likely be greeted with a firm 'no' at best.

I've seen this a few times, where a client will at some point reflect on the cost during the recruitment process and ask for a reduction. Usually, it's at the point of offer. This isn't fair to the recruiter and it isn't fair to any candidates involved in the process either. I've seen clients argue that others are charging less, this being their justification to reduce the fee. However, the reality is that the other recruiter has merely quoted for you. They haven't successfully delivered. Anyone can quote low, and the value of your recruiter's success can't be compared to a quotation that hasn't been actioned and therefore can't be verified as any form of value. Regardless, any negotiation on price should have happened before the recruiter was instructed to commence work on your vacancies.

Communication is key

Once the fees are sorted, the next priority is to create the right business relationship and communication is the key. Many companies expect to be able to send a job specification and a salary range by email and then let the recruitment agency do the rest. To you as a hiring manager, that job specification might seem perfectly self-explanatory. It is one of those situations where you know something so well that it can be hard to understand how someone else would fail to understand too. The truth is that the more information you can provide to your recruiter, the better.

Don't assume that your recruiter knows or fully understands exactly what you want to see from your shortlisted candidates. The more you can tell them about what your applications should include (skills, experience, ideal previous employers, etc.), the more likely you are to receive it. You could even go a step further and share with them what you want to cover and see at interview. This isn't so that recruiters can cheat by falsely prepping candidates. It's about sifting out those that won't meet your criteria, to save you all the time of meeting with candidates that could have been identified as unsuitable.

More importantly, what must be remembered is that agencies are trying to sell your business to prospective candidates. They have to provide reasons why a candidate should choose your company as opposed to your competitors, and only you will have the information needed to do this. Your ideal future candidate is unlikely to be unemployed and waiting for a call. They will need to be convinced, even seduced, by what you have to offer them as a potential employer. They need a reason to believe that your employment opportunity is better than their existing one.

What can you tell the agency about your business that they can use to entice people? How often are your pay reviews? What is the career progression like? What hidden benefits does your company offer? Childcare? Share schemes? Pensions? Welcome bonus? Friendly or supportive team atmosphere? Any awards you have received, either by the company or by individuals? Any endorsements or testimonials you can pass on from other new starters or even clients? This type of useful information isn't going to be found on a simple job specification.

Many HR departments or hiring managers see communication with agencies as a chore or an unwelcome intrusion on their day. It is vital that this attitude is avoided and instead you should encourage all relevant staff to contribute. At the end of the day, the recruiter is only going to ask as many questions as he or she thinks necessary to do a good job for you. It's not because they are nosy or trying to be a pain in your backside, but because they think it just might help!

The more a consultant knows about your business, the better. For that reason, it is a good idea to invite the consultant to visit your business, where you can show them the atmosphere and culture, impress them with your facilities and inspire them to ask even more questions!

The type of relationship you build with your chosen agencies depends on a number of things. If you are a small company and you're only likely to recruit one or two staff members per year, then you aren't looking for the same business relationship as a large company looking for specific, hard-to-find candidates 30 or more times a year. Do what you think is appropriate to communicate with agencies but don't underestimate the value of the information you could give them.

Lastly, it's worth considering that a prospective or target candidate will consider any recruiter who approaches them as a representative of your company. If the recruiter seems unsure or lacks passion in your company, the prospective candidate will probably conclude that it is not for them. Recruiters need the information. Give them the power of the detail and you will get a much better result. By doing this, you will be putting the onus on the agency to provide the best service out there. They have no excuses!

Communication affects your recruiters' motivation

The working day of a consultant is a frantic one, often with dramatically lengthened days to get the work done. They have several demands upon them, all of which are urgent. Because recruitment consultants are so busy, there is a benefit to be had in keeping in touch with the consultant working on your vacancy. Regular communication will keep the focus on your vacancies rather than someone else's.

Above all, agencies are motivated by money. That doesn't mean they are not compassionate or lack care towards people or the quality of their work. However, they have to prioritise in order to have a good chance of hitting their targets. Most recruitment arrangements are based on only invoicing if they are successful in filling the role (contingent recruitment). They will therefore concentrate on the jobs they think they have the best chance of filling. If there is no regular communication from you, they may assume that your need is not as urgent or as important as another's and their attention may be lost to your competition.

Perhaps this might be because some companies like to use agencies as a fallback, engaging the agency and appointing them to look at their vacancy without any real intention to interview any candidate that might be sent through, regardless of their quality or suitability for the role, except as a last resort. Of course, a hirer might engage a recruiter to look at their vacancy while also continuing their own search and there is absolutely nothing wrong with this, nor is there anything wrong with using multiple agencies (within reason and when appropriate). But this is a very different scenario.

Because no fee is paid until the candidate starts employment, businesses can take advantage of agencies in this way. Sadly, it happens more than you might think. Sometimes it is not intentional, but either way, the fact remains that recruitment consultants are used to the uncertainty that they will be left with a withdrawn vacancy after having spent two days or more working on it.

The message is this: make sure your agency knows you are serious. Touch base with them regularly to see how they are getting on or what problems they are having. Tell them why you need this person, when by and what the consequences are for your business if you don't find the person in time. That way, they will know that if they put the work in and concentrate on finding what you are looking for then the odds are that they will end up being able to invoice you!

The importance of (prompt) feedback

Quick feedback on CVs is crucial for three reasons:

1. Finding the *right* person
As I mentioned earlier, it is harder for a recruitment consultant to understand exactly what you are looking for

than you think. What goes without saying for you probably doesn't go without saying for your recruiter! Regardless of their knowledge of the sector, they can't know your specific business needs as well as you do.

Based on the above, the first CVs you receive should be relevant. If they are not up to scratch, they can serve as a benchmark for feedback and improvement. Read through them as quickly as you can and make notes on them. If you are not the decision-maker, ask that person to do this promptly and make them understand the benefit they will receive by doing this and offering useful feedback. Once these notes have been made, call the consultant and talk him or her though the comments. Explain the positives as well as what is bad about the CVs. The consultant will then be able to refine the search with a much more tangible understanding of what they are looking for.

When having this conversation about the CVs, listen to what the consultant has to say about how they are getting on with the search. They will have the best feel for what the market has to offer and can provide information on what you can realistically expect. As you may have found, rarely is there such a thing as the perfect candidate. Instead, it is about compromising a few details in search of the best available candidate you can get. A good consultant will be able to add value by telling you what the market is offering and what you might have to sacrifice. They will also be able to give you a better understanding of the going rate for the specific skill set and experience you require.

2. Keeping the consultant motivated
By responding to any submitted CVs quickly, you are giving the clearest possible message that you are seriously looking and thus further harnessing the commitment of the consultant's time and effort. If CVs are being submitted

and no feedback is offered for a few days (or you don't provide any feedback at all), the consultant can be forgiven for assuming that your vacancy isn't that urgent or that you are not as serious about your recruitment needs.

3. Actually securing the candidate

This point should, and probably does go without saying but... it is so important that it has to be mentioned in this book. More often than not, job applicants will not wait very long for feedback. Due to the fact that most sectors are now operating within a 'skills shortage' (i.e. there are not enough qualified people relative to the number of vacancies), it is the applicant that is in the driving seat, not the employer. They will likely have several options on offer to them, yours being just one of them. In today's fast-paced world, it is often the route of least resistance that candidates end up following. *If your competitor opens a door for them sooner than you do, they are likely to walk through it.* It's then much harder for them to walk through your door when you do eventually get round to inviting them.

Individuals are empowered to choose the best career option that suits them. If they don't receive feedback quickly, they will move on and apply for other things. Or worse, your competition will make them feel more valued by responding quicker, and you will have lost your very rare, high-quality applicant.

Feedback doesn't have to be definitive. If a candidate is of potential interest, feed that back to your recruiter and explain why. If you are waiting for something to happen (or not happen) internally, then tell them as much as you can, and why you can't move forward just yet. Give them a realistic time frame if you can. Get your recruiter to do what they can to keep your potential candidate warm, without being dishonest to them.

Try and get a date in the diary for an interview as quickly as possible, even if it is a way off. If the diary is proving difficult to manage, perhaps arrange an informal phone chat, even if simply to retain the candidate's focus and interest. A good consultant will do their best to regularly liaise with submitted candidates for the role in an effort to keep their interest and attention on your vacancy, but the slower the feedback, the harder this is for them to achieve for you.

I can't make this point strongly enough: time kills all hires. Businesses and hiring managers that act quickly win over those that take their time to book people in for interviews. Every time!

There is a good chance that you have been chased by a recruiter before. They know that time kills all hires, and don't want you to fall foul of it. It's bad news for both you and the recruiter. If they are working on a contingent basis (i.e. they only get to invoice you when a candidate starts in a role), then this is where they see their hard work disappearing down the proverbial toilet. Sadly, that is a sure-fire way to lose their focus from your business and onto your competitors.

I know that this is a challenge to achieve as hiring managers have their day job to worry about first. But it doesn't change these facts.

Communicating the offer

By this stage of the process, if your recruiter isn't pushing for quick movement, they really should be. Too often, I hear of clients who have interviewed someone that they intend to offer the job to, however they prefer to wait. Our research into the reasons behind this has uncovered a feeling that they don't want to appear too keen. They have a feeling that offering too quickly may somehow reduce their chances of securing the candidate into the role.

My experience and data tell me the exact opposite. Attitudes around this area have changed significantly over the years. In today's modern world, egos play a significant part in recruitment. Delaying on making an offer will instead likely be interpreted as though you, the hirer, might be unsure about their suitability. This might be a confidence blow. It might also make them lean towards another company that appears keener to welcome them with open arms. At the very least, it gives your competition more time to close them ahead of you.

Time kills all hires. This could never be truer than at this stage of the recruitment process. If you've decided, act quickly and make good use of the opportunity you have to make the candidate feel welcomed and special. Get your working relationship off to the best possible start.

Honesty and trust

Have you ever found it difficult to trust your agency to tell you the absolute truth, or felt that you weren't getting the whole story? Have you ever wondered whether an agency has inflated salary requirements for all the CVs they send over? Have you ever felt that you are being put under pressure to make a decision on an offer, for no other reason than the agenda of the recruiter?

My belief is that this is largely a thing of the past, at least for all but a small percentage of recruiters. Regardless, this shouldn't happen and there are lots of good agencies out there with the highest of ethical and moral standards. If you get the feeling that lack of honesty is the case, then it might be that they are not the right agency with whom to build a long-term relationship.

However, to ensure you receive an honest and trustworthy service, tell them that you want to build this kind of trusting relationship and that as long as you receive this sort of service, you will respond to the information given in return.

Recruitment consultants may well tell a slight untruth or exaggerate a point just to get a reaction. An example might be an exaggeration on how likely a candidate is to withdraw their application, if the client doesn't speed up their response and book them in for an interview. Some recruiters might use an elaboration of the truth here in the hope of getting the hirer to book the interview faster. Albeit this will usually be in the interest of the client and candidate, as well as their own agenda. If the recruiter knows they are under scrutiny to be honest, they will likely be more truthful. Equally, if they know that you will listen to a concern and react accordingly without them having to overdramatise things, you are well on your way to achieving a transparent and harmonious working relationship.

In summary, both parties need to feel as though they are working together and helping each other to achieve a mutually beneficial goal. Life gets so much easier and more prosperous for both parties when this level of working relationship is reached.

Strategy

Number of agencies

The more agencies you use, the higher the chance of finding the right person... right? Wrong! Look at this situation through the eyes of an agency. If you are competing against ten other agencies to fill a vacancy, there is a very high chance that the time spent on this will be wasted. So, by allowing multiple agencies to work on your vacancies, all you are really ensuring is a lack of commitment from all your providers. The service you receive will likely be rather poor and your faith in the recruitment industry will drop considerably.

Instead, harness the attention and focus of your providers by telling them that they have the vacancy alongside only one or perhaps two other agencies. The exact number will of course depend on the nature, variety and volume of your recruitment needs. Whatever the number, reassure them that you will say no to other agencies asking whether they can work on your vacancies. Make it clear that as long as they work hard and do a good job, they have a very high chance of being able to invoice you.

Exclusivity?

The subject of exclusivity doesn't come up enough in recruitment. The traditional model is that a hiring business will go out to multiple businesses. That could be two or three. I've also come across larger organisations that have well over 100 suppliers. How can you possibly build a working relationship with that many suppliers?

The recruitment sector is quite extraordinary really. I can't think of another service-based industry that works in the same way. Imagine a scenario where you need your tax return done. Instead of picking one accountant, you go out to multiple accountants, send them all your figures and say, 'The first one to get my accounts finished and returned to me will get paid. The rest of you… tough luck!'

In a hypothetical world where you could find accountants to agree to this, you would be incentivising them to do a 'rush job' of your accounts rather than doing them properly. Plus, you would also be asking them to take on work and work hard, with a very good chance that the work they do will be in vain. The chances are that the good ones would pass, while only the desperate ones consider picking it up.

That's effectively what is happening in the world of recruitment. There are plenty of exceptions, but this is the way the majority of the recruitment sector operates. When a hiring company tells the recruiter that they are one of four agencies, they 'hear' that they are only being given 25% of the client's commitment. So that's what they can afford to give in return. The trouble for the client is, in this instance 4 x 25% does not equate to 100% of the results. It often amounts to no more than 25% of what might have been possible, if they had given a single, quality recruiter the full commitment. Those four agencies are all doing a similar, partial job. Collectively, that still amounts to less than 100% focus from one really good agency that knows that it is entirely on them to get the vacancy filled.

So, the question is: 'What if my one agency fails to find the people we need?'

Well, by giving that agency your commitment and showing them that it is worth their while – assuming you've chosen a good quality and relevant recruitment agency – this will result in much more commitment and motivation from them in return. You've made it safe for them to do the job that they wish they could do all the time.

Your chosen exclusive supplier will also have a sense of commitment to you to get the job done, given you have granted them the respect of assigning them your exclusive business. They will know that you have no backup and will suffer if they can't deliver. They won't be able to reassure themselves that someone else will come to your rescue. It's 100% on them.

The chances of them getting you a good result are greatly increased in this instance.

You also have the option of a safety mechanism that works for both parties. For most exclusive agreements, I would recommend that the exclusivity lasts for a specified period of time, per vacancy. You could, for instance, stipulate that your supplier has three weeks of exclusivity on new vacancies, before you then offer up the vacancy to a second-tier group of agencies.

This way, you get all the benefits of an exclusivity arrangement, but in the event that they can't deliver, you have only lost three weeks. The time frame should vary depending on the nature of the role and industry you are recruiting for. A temporary warehouse operative might take significantly less time, while an operations director might take significantly longer to do a thorough job. I believe this is an under-utilised technique.

It also has one last, but potentially very significant, benefit: bargaining power. An agency may be willing to reduce their fees in return for exclusivity on the role. After all, their odds are much improved to fill the vacancy. Their likelihood of being able to invoice you after a job well done is increased, while the risk of their efforts being wasted is reduced. It may well be that they are willing to concede on the rate slightly, or perhaps even significantly.

Of course, using a small, select collection of recruiters, or a single and exclusive recruiter will only work well if you choose the right supplier or suppliers in the first place.

Choosing the right agencies

There is an endless choice of agencies out there. Depending on the industry you are in, you may already be unlucky enough to be receiving several sales calls a day from different agencies, trying to get a vacancy or two to work on. You may, in fact, have become an expert at getting rid of agencies very quickly: an important skill for the sake of your own time management! (We'll cover how you can protect your time from these unwanted enquiries later in the book.) It is difficult to see clearly in such a busy industry, so how do you find the right ones?

The obvious place to start is by looking at the agencies you have already used. Companies that already know your business will have an advantage and ultimately save you time. However, a potential downside is that they may already have a formed approach to working on your vacancies and that approach might not be as efficient as it could be. In some ways, you might find it more difficult to get the business relationship you are aiming for with these pre-established companies. You might find that it takes more effort to get them to abolish any misunderstandings they have about your company.

Another way to identify good recruitment agencies is to seek out referrals. What experiences have your business customers (if you are B2B) had with agencies? Equally, do your business suppliers know of any particularly good agencies or consultants?

There are many different types of agencies out there. They vary in size, speciality, ability, diversity, location coverage and candidate seniority. To reduce the number of companies you are dealing with, you may want to consider a company that can cater for a number of your requirements. The more diverse your own business, the harder it will be to find suppliers that can supply all the different types and categories of staff that you might require. For a more complex company, it might be worth segmenting the recruitment for different aspects of the business. For example, offer your blue-collar vacancies to three suitable agencies and your white-collar positions to three different agencies. Make sure it is known to all companies that they are still only competing against two other agencies for the relevant vacancies that they have, for example.

Having said the above, the market trend these days is what I would refer to as 'inch wide, mile deep'. Ideally, you are looking for a highly specialist recruiter that knows all the players and corners of the industry. These are the recruiters who are getting the best results and offering the best customer experience and working relationships. They really have their finger on the pulse of your specific areas of interest. On the flip side, be wary of anyone who claims that they can fill any type of vacancy, whether that be an individual or an entire firm. You really want to avoid having them learn about what you need on your time. They are supposed to be saving you time rather than being a burden on it.

Types of recruitment

For permanent recruitment, there are four core formats of recruitment, as follows:

Contingency
If you have a small number of vacancies each year you may prefer to take a contingency approach to recruitment. Effectively, for each individual vacancy you are agreeing terms separately, from a fresh sheet of paper. You can choose the agencies to use based on their own specialities.

There are downsides to this approach though. Agencies will not already know your business. It might be harder to negotiate on fees if there is no mention of repeat business. You won't know what sort of service you might receive. Of course, there is nothing stopping you from returning to the same agency or consultant each time, even if you only recruit very rarely.

PSL (Preferred Supplier List)
A PSL (Preferred Supplier List) is a great way of clearly defining and communicating your intentions and giving your chosen suppliers a tangible reason to concentrate on your vacancies rather than someone else's.

Firstly, for reasons already mentioned, it is important not to put too many agencies on your PSL. Secondly, you need to make sure that all your likely staffing requirements are catered for. Make sure that the assembled list of agencies can supply you with all the different types of staff you might need, as a collective.

The formality of a Preferred Supplier List has several advantages. It is a tangible success for an agency to be placed on a PSL. You are offering them something (a place on your very select PSL) while asking in return for improved terms and a commitment to place your vacancies higher up on their priority list. You are also tying them into a predefined period of time, meaning that they are also likely to receive future business from you. Aside from these benefits, your suppliers know that they are protected by the PSL. It means that you will not be taking on other agencies through sales calls.

There is also a significant side advantage to having a PSL. A PSL gives you a very efficient way of getting rid of agencies making sales calls. 'Sorry, we have a PSL already and we are contracted to using these agencies only. Thanks for calling. Goodbye!'

So, what happens if your PSL fails to find you the person you are looking for? Not to worry. You can still go to other agencies at a later date if you do not receive the right candidate. It is advisable to predefine a time frame. For example: 'The PSL has three working weeks, after which we reserve the right to enlist a second-tier group of agencies to work on the vacancy.' In all likelihood, if an agency is going to find you the right person, they will have found it within three weeks. Obviously, you can set this time frame to be appropriate for the nature of the roles that you are recruiting for. The typical type of person you are looking for will dictate the amount of time in which you can reasonably expect your PSL to come up with the right person.

You may well be thinking, 'Three weeks, that's a big delay to our recruitment process' and you are correct. However, from experience, I can confidently say that, by making this sort of commitment to a small group of agencies, investing time into them so they have a working knowledge of your business, and making sure you've collated the right group of agencies, you will be finding much better candidates for your roles, much more quickly in general. Of course, there is always a chance the PSL may fail to find you what you need. However, at least you have already hedged your bets by giving it to a group of suppliers instead of just one.

Master Vendor/Managed Agent

A Master Vendor or Managed Agent agreement is where you liaise with just one agency. It is then up to them to ensure that your vacancies are filled effectively. If they can fill them all to the right standard on their own, then that's all well and good. If this is not the case, then they may well engage other agencies on your behalf.

This is different to the exclusivity arrangement we described earlier. In that instance, you are effectively working on a contingency basis, but choosing to work with just one single supplier, which will work to fill your vacancy on their own. A Master Vendor or Managed Agent is an exclusive supplier from your perspective, though they may well work with multiple suppliers to help them fill the role. The difference is that all the liaising will be done by them, and they remain your single point of contact. It typically works well for ongoing recruitment needs, or volume requirements where you might need regular, differing skill sets. A contingency-based exclusivity deal would work better with one-off vacancies as appropriate.

Your favourite and most trusted agency will know the industry well and they will know which other agencies to engage with or avoid. In this scenario, you the hirer are relieved of the hassle of having to communicate with several agencies. It is the Master Vendor agency's responsibility to pre-vet all applications from other agencies before passing them on to you. In some instances, your accounts department will also only receive invoices from the one agency. The fee will then be passed on, either in part or in full depending on the agreement between the two agencies. The beauty of it is that it isn't your concern, and you have the advantage of a single point of contact but the benefit of a potential army of suppliers.

A Master Vendor agreement is the most rigid and high-level agreement. They are normally drawn up as a formal, legal document and will govern your recruitment practice for a fairly long period of time. The potential advantages are extremely significant: continuity of communication, detail, quality, fee transfers, etc. It all adds up to a potentially slick recruitment process. It may also work out to be more cost-effective based on discounts offered in return for such commitment and/or volume from your business.

Equally, there are a number of notable risks which need to be looked into carefully, before this option is chosen. You are placing a lot of faith in one recruitment company, which carries inherent risks. What would happen, for example, if their best consultant left the business? Perhaps the one individual with whom you had built that rapport up and trusted. What happens if you become unsatisfied with the company's performance while tied into a long-term exclusivity deal?

Therefore, it may be worth thinking about setting certain contractual expectations or key performance indicators (KPIs), that would allow you to be released from the contract should you not be getting what you need. We will cover how to monitor performance of your chosen agency or agencies, and how to outline your expectations later in the book.

Head hunting/retained search/executive search

This form of recruitment is usually more suited to the senior appointments, though many of the techniques used for and devised for this level of recruitment are now also being used on mid-level, hard-to-find candidates.

In essence, this type of recruitment is done with a single, exclusive recruitment firm. A 'retainer fee' is paid at the initial stages, and this buys you the time of the recruitment firm. They will use that time to conduct a search process, based on your exact criteria, to identify the most suitable people for your role. Further fees are then paid at later stages. These structures vary from firm to firm and may well be negotiable, but here is an outline of a typical structure:

- One third of the fee up front (the retainer fee)
- One third of the fee at interview shortlisting stage
- One third of the fee on completion (successfully hired into the role)

It is a more involved and intensive process so it will usually cost a little more overall. However, your odds of ultimately successfully recruiting a star performer are usually significantly higher.

As I've mentioned, this form of recruitment was devised for the most senior of roles initially – probably £100k salaries upwards. However, as skills shortages have worsened in most sectors and as the war on talent attraction intensifies, this option has increased in popularity and effectiveness for mid-level roles too and is worth considering for highly skilled roles or mid-level management roles.

This type of recruitment is very popular with recruitment agencies as well and is a great way of ensuring your role gets the utmost attention and the best chance of success. To you, this option has many pros and cons relative to other options. Having paid a retainer, you will be purchasing the attention, focus and skills of the recruitment company, will little or no danger of the vacancy being neglected. A good agency is unlikely to take on such an assignment if they lack confidence in their ability to find the right person for you. They would not want to be in a position where they are financially committed to search for something they can't find. Nevertheless, it is good practice to have that conversation with your recruiter about what happens if they can't find what you are looking for.

The negative of this option is that you will need to invest up front, at least in part. If you do end up being disappointed with the level of service or results, there are fewer options, at least without losing that initial investment.

Invariably though, retained search companies are usually a bit more professional and effective than those that don't offer such things. It isn't suitable for all vacancy types, but may be a worthwhile consideration for certain roles, especially if you have a willing agency with which you already have a good working relationship.

Subscription services and embedded recruitment solutions

The 'Netflix model' (of recurring monthly fees for a known and trusted service) has swept through so many industries with great success. It suits the modern world perfectly. People rarely 'buy' new cars these days. Instead, they lease them. You can now do this for a sofa or a fridge, your accounting fees, or your car servicing.

The recruitment industry has been slow to adopt such models. These service options do exist though, and since

2020, I've seen a much more accelerative uptake. The reality is this: the best suppliers are the ones that are leading the way on these types of services.

If you want the absolute best from a recruitment supplier, it is worth some consideration towards retaining them on a monthly or ongoing basis. This will only be suitable for those businesses that have an ongoing recruitment need. It makes no sense for a single hire. You need to find a solution that suits your needs and variances over a period of time (or have your supplier design a custom one for you).

When moving to a subscription model, many suppliers will start to give you more favourable terms, flexibilities and prices, often significantly so. You may also get a higher quality of individual recruiter(s) working on your account, an exclusive or dedicated point of contact or any manner of other useful benefits. You should also be looking for a higher level of data insights, analysis and reporting, together with some regular consultancy from a senior member of their team thrown into the package.

If there is one single thing that affects the quality and results that you get from recruitment services, it is the quality of your working relationship. If you have the mutual trust and respect, and are committed to helping each other and working together, you'll likely see results go through the roof. This is the nub of the reason why subscription models can work so powerfully.

The nature of your hiring needs will determine the specifics of the subscription model that will suit you, so it would be difficult to offer detailed advice about what might work for you specifically.

Other recruitment products and services

Aside from the above, your recruiter may have other options for you to consider. These might include:

Advertise Only – A more affordable alternative, but a bit more labour intensive on your part. They can write the advert for you, as well as post and manage the live adverts. You would likely need to work though the applications yourself.

Outsourcing – Perhaps you feel that you need an additional human resource (or several), but don't have the capacity internally to hire, train and manage them. Some recruiters can offer you a dedicated, experienced and well-trained human resource for you. They can be 'plugged in' to your existing team, either onsite or remotely, and appear to be an embedded member of your team rather than an external provider. This can be great for your recruiter branding.

Out-Placement Services – If you are unfortunate enough to have to make redundancies or cutbacks of any kind, some recruitment businesses will offer an out-placement service. That recruiter then takes on the responsibility of assisting your outgoing staff to help them find a suitable alternative job. This service could include things like a free CV review, a consultation session on what their best options might be, a salary guide, and so on.

Out-placement services have been seen by employers as a caring and positive step. If you can demonstrate that you are being proactive with your efforts to help people, this can considerably improve the mood at a time when it will be being tested. Remaining staff will also likely have some respect for the fact that you are doing what you can to help. The best part of this service is that, dependent on your sector, many recruiters will do this for you for zero charge. The benefit to them is that they will be getting an introduction to skilled people which they will hopefully be able to place with other existing clients.

Consultation

Whatever model or service type you settle on with your recruitment provider or providers, assuming you've chosen those providers well, they should have a wealth of information that can benefit you. If they are worth their salt, they may likely have valuable insight and information from which you can benefit. The hint is in the job title: Recruitment Consultant. All too often, this job title gets given out to mere CV shufflers. If you can find a good one (whatever their title), you have an opportunity to engage them on more than just the blinkered task of finding candidates.

It pays dividends to regularly ask your trusted suppliers for consultative advice. They should have a wealth of diverse information about what is working in your sector, what your competitors are doing that you aren't, and many other valuable insights.

They should also have a strong vantage point to gauge the health and virtues of your 'employer brand'. Do you have a strong reputation in the industry, among your target candidate market? Or are discussions taking place that might concern you? Your true employer brand is what people will say about you once you've left the room. That can be very different from what they would say to your face. Your recruiter(s) should be hearing this and feeding back to you.

The reality, though, is that they may not feel immediately comfortable to give you this type of information. That means it is up to you to make it safe for them to do so. Don't just ask a brief question about your reputation in the market. Tell them in clear terms that you want a 'warts and all' reflection of your employer brand. The good AND the bad.

What else could you think of that you'd potentially stand to learn, if you ask the right questions? Perhaps they could help you with:

- salary benchmarking
- benefits package reflections
- interview processes
- the best interview questions that others are asking
- probation periods
- onboarding processes that are proving to be the most effective
- training that other companies are providing/who the best external trainers are.

I'm sure you can think of many more. If they're good recruiters, they will probably already know. If not, then they are perfectly positioned to find out for you.

Terms of business

I am not a lawyer and none of the below should be considered as legal advice. This section is aimed at giving you some concepts and areas to think about. I would always advocate that business terms should be written by someone with the appropriate qualifications.

The business terms should cover off a variety of different and complex legislation so are unlikely to be a brief document. There are several common contractual stumbling blocks, and in this section, we look to identify them and mitigate the risk of any issues.

Again, in this section we are focusing on recruitment for permanent roles. Contracts for temporary or contract roles are very different.

Get the business terms sorted early

First things first: any agency who doesn't offer you a comprehensive contract or 'Terms of Business' document is NOT worth working with. There is absolutely no excuse for this. Additionally, this should be offered up at the outset, prior to them commencing work on your vacancies.

Sometimes, you will have been sent a CV in a speculative manner and out of the blue. This is a common way for recruitment agencies to approach new clients. If that CV or candidate profile is of potential interest and you wish to move forward or learn more, make sure you get terms agreed before arranging an interview. It will save you the awkwardness of trying to negotiate when the agency knows that they have something that you really want. It won't improve your ability to strike a fair deal and will add an element of lumpiness and uncertainty to your recruitment process. In these situations, the candidate will quite often pick up on this awkwardness, potentially giving them the impression that you are a less professional or desirable prospective employer.

Managing the overlap of suppliers

The other challenge potentially facing you when working with multiple agencies, is that those agencies' terms will all differ slightly, and may not work well alongside each other. This is especially true when it comes to the issue of candidate representation and ownership.

It is common for the same candidate to be introduced by multiple suppliers. The worst possible outcome here is that, having taken on a new employee, your business is liable to pay more than one fee from more than one agency for a single candidate. I've seen this happen many times, unfortunately.

You can see how this might happen. You get sent a CV from one agency, but it goes into your junk folder or you miss it somehow. You then get the same candidate from a different supplier. An interview is arranged through the second supplier and you successfully hire that person. Somewhere along the line the first supplier discovers that you have employed the candidate that they believe they have introduced to you. Their business terms state that an introduction is triggered by the details of a candidate being sent via email, for example. Subsequently, you end up with two invoices for a single candidate. The other agency's terms emphasise the introduction being defined as the arranging of an interview. Both would legitimately apply in this scenario.

This issue is a real one and stems from the details of how a supplier contractually determines that they are due a fee. This is again something that is crucial for you to fully understand. There are many different approaches out there and they don't always work alongside each other.

The good news is that most businesses are professional enough to recognise that it makes no sense for a business to be charged twice for a single introduction and they are likely to come to an arrangement in this instance. However, it may still be a fairly labour-intensive process with one agency arguing that they somehow have more of an ownership over the candidate than the other. You don't want to put yourself in this position if at all possible.

In the scenario where you have agreed multiple terms with different agencies, you have the option of requesting an additional clause or addendum being added to all existing terms, that reads something similar to one of the following options:

1. In the event that the same candidate is put forward by more than one agency, the first agency to submit the candidate will have representation of that candidate, so long as they can prove that they had the permission of the candidate to submit their details to XYZ Company.
2. In the event that the same candidate is put forward by more than one agency, the agency that arranged the interview will have representation of that candidate, so long as they can prove that they had the permission of the candidate to submit their details to XYZ Company.
3. In the event that the same candidate is put forward by more than one agency, it shall be the candidate's decision who they wish to be represented by. In this instance, a representative of XYZ company will approach

the candidate and discuss with them which agency they would like to be represented by. The result of this conversation will be final.
4. In the event that the same candidate is put forward by more than one agency, the fee will be shared equally between them.

Each of these have their pros and cons. Option 1 emphasises speed. Sometimes speed comes at the expense of quality. It is not uncommon for low-quality agencies to send CV submissions without even speaking to the candidate beforehand, and sometimes your best supplier will have submitted the same candidate slightly later, but having done a thorough job of screening them for suitability for your company. Nonetheless, it also ensures that you will not be sent candidates who haven't been through a detailed pre-screen. That's why the last bit of Option 1 is essential. If the agency can't prove that they had permission to send this CV prior to sending it, they would have no contractual grounds to charge a fee. Of the four options, this would be my preferred option when dealing with multiple suppliers.

Option 2 is my second favourite. It is clean, clear-cut, and harder to misinterpret. Equally though, you may struggle to get your suppliers to agree to this.

Putting the decision in the candidate's hands (Option 3) might appear like a good idea. After all, they are the ones who will really know which agency has truly represented them and done a professional job. However, this puts the candidate in a position where each agency will be trying to persuade them. It can get very messy. I think it ultimately looks unfavourably on everyone, including you as the end hirer. It rarely ends well for anyone unfortunately.

Sharing the fee equally might again appear to be a good choice, as per Option 4. Yet the reality is that one agency will have done a better job than the other. Neither is likely to be happy with this, including you, as you will have two agencies to liaise with about the candidate's onboarding, start date, plus two (smaller) invoices to pay. This option usually ends up just as messy as Option 3.

This issue is one of the more complicated potential pitfalls, but it is rare and shouldn't scare you or put you off. It is only likely to trouble those that are recruiting in fairly high volumes. Be clear on exactly how your agencies are defining an introduction, or what the qualification is to legally be entitled to invoice you. With this clear in your mind, you should be able to successfully navigate around this issue.

Build your own standardised terms

A simple way around this is to insist that you have your own business terms, that each of your suppliers sign. (We'll cover this in more detail later in the book.) It is the only way to have real clarity on all agreements, when working with multiple suppliers. When doing this though, make sure that they are a fair set of operational terms, to ensure the continued support of your suppliers. You can still have some flexibility of negotiation within the one template. For example, you could still agree different fees, rebate periods or payment days, so long as the mechanics of the agreement are standardised.

Fees

We've touched on this under negotiation techniques, but this is an obvious area where the business terms need to be unambiguous. Make sure you understand it clearly. Is it a percentage of the candidate's starting salary? Does this vary depending on the salary value? Is it a fixed fee? If one of these options suits you better, don't be afraid to request it, so long as it is still a fair price for the service that you are expecting to receive (or the value of the solution to the recruitment problem you have).

Refunds or rebates

We've explored this clause under the Negotiation section of this book. Nevertheless, it is a crucial aspect of the business terms and must be clear.

Suitability checks

There are several legal or best practice responsibilities that fall to the recruiter and which should be included in the business terms. This is especially true when recruiting for people to work with young or vulnerable people. The purpose of this book is not to offer legal advice, purely practical advice. So, I will stop short of fully disclosing these responsibilities, but encourage you to look at this section of the agreement carefully and ensure that it includes what you would expect.

Who produces the terms of business or contract?

Traditionally, if you engage with a recruitment agency, you would be agreeing to their business terms. Increasingly though, businesses are requesting that this is flipped, and the recruitment agency must sign the client's terms. This is common with large organisations and is more prudent for them where they are recruiting in high volumes and/ or working with larger numbers of suppliers. Having all of their suppliers on the same terms creates a much less complicated scenario for them and creates a fair and equal playing field for their suppliers.

Those advantages also extend to smaller businesses too, though they are perhaps less important.

The advantage to signing your supplier's terms of business is that you don't have to go to the trouble and expense of having a solicitor draw up terms for you. The disadvantage is that, if working with several suppliers, perhaps as part of a PSL, you may have varying agreements with each party, adding a level of inconsistency and confusion to your overall recruitment processes.

I would suggest that it is worth considering having your own terms drawn up to be used with suppliers at the point at which you start running into logistical issues of having multiple suppliers on different agreements, including fees, rebate periods, payment terms, etc. Fix it only if it is actually broken, so to speak.

If you do go down this route, expect a bit of resistance from some of your suppliers. It may be worth engaging with them to try and find a consensus, before deciding on the terms. You may also choose to have a standard basic template but with variable clauses. For example, if your concern was over rebates, your own terms should standardise, clarify and solve this issue for you, while still giving you the option to have different suppliers on different fee structures or payment terms, etc.

Having your suppliers on your own set of business terms gives you a significantly higher level of overall control and consistency. This may well be worth considering if you are running into contractual issues and complications. It works best as part of a PSL (Preferred Supplier List) review and rollout, and/or tender process.

If you can't, or don't want to, have all suppliers on the same fee or rebate structure, then that is absolutely fine. It is more important to standardise things like candidate ownership, service levels and standards, etc. than it is to standardise fees, for example.

When drawing up your own terms, you can either approach a solicitor to do this for you or seek out a suitable template that you can then customise relatively easily. Organisations like the Recruitment & Employment Confederation (REC) and The Recruitment Network (TRN) will have such templates that their members can make use of.

Monitoring recruiter performance and setting expectations

Winning your business and getting the go ahead to work on your important vacancies is only the start for your recruitment supplier. This is where the real work starts, and they need to prove to you that they should remain as your supplier.

It is important that both parties have an understanding of expectations. It is just as important that these expectations are reasonable ones, relative to the nature of your industry and the skill sets you are recruiting for. If you are working with a small number of suppliers, you may wish to engage them in the process of setting these expectations. If you are operating a PSL, you will likely need a 'standardised' service level agreement (SLA), which you can use to monitor the performance of all of your suppliers.

An SLA is simply an agreement with outlines, expectations and responsibilities of both the recruiter and the end hirer, whether that be the end hiring manager or the HR department responsible (or both). An SLA would likely include both clear KPIs as well as what expectations there are in the event of mistakes or disappointments. SLAs have been proven to enhance the candidate experience, as well as dramatically reduce the time to hire, so long as they are used proactively. So, consider including one in your agreement with your recruitment suppliers.

What expectations should be outlined?

This is dependent on what you actually want from your recruitment suppliers and what is important to you. For example, are you looking to outsource your recruitment for the main agenda of saving you time? Or are you prepared to commit as much time to the process as needed because hiring is the most important thing for the key objectives of your business?

Typical measures could include the following. In some cases, I have provided example percentages, but these are purely for illustration and you'll need to discuss what the right percentages are for your business and your supplier(s):

- 'Vacancy release to CV Submission' lead time targets
  o Only suitable for industries that have sufficient volumes of interest. For some skill sets, it may take weeks to find just one suitable applicant. For others, it will be reasonable to expect a shortlist of three CVs sent within two working days or less.

- Time to Hire target
  o Similar to above, but a target for the time taken from vacancy release through to new hire start date.

- CVs Submitted to Interviews Booked target
  o In the form of a percentage or ratio. For example, minimum 75% of submitted candidates to be invited for and successfully attend an interview.

- Drop Outs/Interview Cancellations/Offer Refusal limits
  o Offer acceptance requirement – e.g. minimum 80%.
  o Interview attendance requirement – e.g. not less than 95%.

- Compliance
  o With compliance targets, you may have certain elements which are specific to your sector. Either

way, any compliance expectations should be outlined as not less than 100%.

- CVs Submitted to Placements Started
  o E.g. not less than 20%.

Importantly, most of these targets will be affected by yourself and your company, as much as they are affected by the recruiter. For example, if the 'Offers Accepted' percentage target is falling short, could this be because they are sending the wrong candidates? Or could it be because your firm isn't appearing to be attractive enough to those candidates? Perhaps they didn't feel a rapport with the interviewers, or the financial package wasn't strong enough in comparison to your competition?

For these sorts of reasons, it is also well worth considering setting your own KPIs and agreeing these with your supplier(s). Indeed, they may request or even insist on this as part of the arrangement. Examples could include:

- Maximum two working days to respond and provide feedback on submitted CVs.

- Maximum two working days to provide feedback on interviews, even if it is not yet a definitive answer one way or the other. (Perhaps giving the recruiter something to keep your candidate warm while you interview other applicants.)

- Interview to be booked within a maximum of two weeks of receiving the application.

Both parties need to recognise their role in achieving your hiring goals. It is again why the targets need to be set appropriately, such that they can be used as a fair and accurate measure of performance.

At the very least, it will give you a measure of how each of your recruiters is performing relative to each other.

The importance of regular review meetings

From my experience, ALL of the high-performing, high-volume recruitment relationships involve regular review meetings. This is a classic 'important but not urgent' task, that too often gets overlooked. As a result, it is your recruitment results that suffer. These meetings can be as often as required but I would recommend monthly meetings as a minimum in the early stages.

A regular, pre-booked meeting holds both parties accountable to doing what they agreed in the previous meeting. It gives both parties an opportunity to discuss challenges before they become real problems. It gives everyone more clarity and motivation to get the job done. This has to be one of the easiest hacks in this book. If nothing else, please take this one away with you.

As with any meeting, make sure you have a structure and/or agenda to keep it time efficient and on point. Don't be afraid to tell your recruiter what you want to see more or less of, and what your pain points are, even if you don't think they have a solution. They might surprise you. Monitoring recruiter performance is not enough. You need to communicate it too.

Recruiter league tables

This is a fun one!

For some reason, I have always found hiring businesses to be less than forthcoming with details about how a particular recruiter is performing relative to their competition. Stereotypically speaking, recruiters are competitive beasts! They have an inner need to know where they sit in the performance hierarchy of your supplier base. More often than not, companies are only willing to tell them something vague, like 'You're doing OK' or 'You're in our top three'.

Being open and honest with your recruitment suppliers will only serve to further and strengthen your relationship. If they are your number one, tell them that they are your number one. The usual reaction to that is that they work even harder on your account because they are excited about being number one, and terrified of losing the top spot. If they are number two, tell them that, and give them some reasoning as to why, or what they would need to do to be your number one. They will absolutely accept and relish the challenge. Additionally, if they are towards the bottom, definitely tell them. They need to know. They might be under the false pretence that they are doing much better than they are.

Of course, there are lots of ways to judge performance. It might be the number of successful placements, the length of time that those placements stay in post, or the speed with which they get you your first CV for a new role. It might just be based on your personal experience of what they are like to work with, perhaps a nice balance of chasing you enough, but never too much.

My point is this: feedback is the breakfast of champions. If you give them the feedback and tell them where they stand in the pecking order, you will get a positive response. If you don't, they almost certainly shouldn't be on your supplier list anyway.

Way back when some of my colleagues were working for Ford in Dagenham, Ford ran an open and published supplier league table. It was based purely on the number of contractors working for them at a time. The recruiters absolutely loved this. To have transparent and almost live information on where they were relative to competition; that was a really smart move. Since then, I've talked to many clients about implementing something similar. Only a small percentage have taken the idea forward, but good results and feedback came from all those that did.

Internal and external recruiters... best of frenemies?

Does your business have its own internal recruiter, or recruitment team? Do you still rely on external recruitment services to fill the gaps?

If the answer to both of these questions is yes, then it is time well-invested to think about how the relationship between these two is set up. These two separate entities can either help or hinder each other. I have seen plenty of examples of internal and external teams working in harmony together, focusing on shared goals and making a positive impact on hiring for the company. I've also witnessed examples where they are at war with each other, distrusting of each other, in fierce competition and doing what they can to hinder each other's progress. The latter is good for absolutely no one, especially your business and its goal for headcount growth.

It all depends on the structures that are created in the middle. Those structures will depend on the extent to which you want your team filling most or all of your vacancies directly. If this is a realistic goal, your structures should look a bit different to a scenario where you know that you will need significant assistance from an external supplier or suppliers.

Regardless, there is a good chance that you will want to reward your internal team more so than external agencies, if they achieve hires on their own. The trick is to make sure that this reward is not at the cost of the overall goal.

Here are some thoughts and options:

Same incentives, regardless
Some businesses offer their internal recruiters the same bonus, commission, recognition, points, etc. regardless of whether they fill it directly or via an external recruiter. This promotes collaboration and is likely to gain the most progress towards filling all roles as quickly and accurately as possible.

Reduced incentive
Some businesses offer a reduced incentive for placements involving an external recruiter. This at least still encourages collaboration and includes a message that it is OK to go externally. Significantly though, it places a greater focus on getting the job done in-house, if that is important to you.

Nominated vacancies, or vacancy categories
Another option is to determine which vacancies your team can go externally for, and for those vacancies only, to still offer an equal (or reduced) incentive.

Split performance bonuses
We have seen businesses offer two different bonus pots at the same time. One for filling a set percentage or volume of vacancies overall, and the other bonus being paid out for having filled a set percentage or volume of placements internally. This can work nicely as it incentivises the appropriate use of external recruiters, but they will naturally look to fill the vacancies themselves where they can. At the same time, your recruiters will still be receiving the internal assistance that they need to successfully get the job done.

Incentives are an important factor in filling your vacancies. Whether they are internal or external, recruiters will generally be significantly influenced by the incentives. Their efforts and actions will go wherever you incentivise them to go.

It could well be that your business's aim is to do away with the reliance on external recruitment services altogether. After all, that does seem to be on the agenda for the majority of HR and recruitment directors. That's a great aim, and some of these structures will work in this scenario, where you have a need in the short term, but still want to incentivise your internal team to make consistent progress towards being independent. Just beware of being too aggressive with your incentives internally, if you aren't yet at the point where you can do without external recruiters. Make sure your internal team can still win, when utilising an appropriate level of external assistance.

How to deal with (potentially high volumes of) recruiter enquiries

A few times before, I've heard clients talk of completely unmanageable levels of recruiter enquiries and sales calls. 'We've had over 20 calls today, alone!' How do you deal with that, without it becoming a massive drain on your time? We are all time-poor these days and our time must be protected, right?

If you are proactively on the lookout for new suppliers, then these calls might be welcome. Even then, it can often be said that the best recruiters are doing the least new client prospecting, as they already have great clients on board. If you are looking for new suppliers, you're better off doing your own research. Better yet, seek referrals and testimonials for good ones, perhaps from similar businesses to your own.

Let the recruiter deal with the problem

If you were to appoint a single supplier or Master Vendor supplier (with all the likely and potential benefits associated, as already discussed), you would have the option of using that agency as a shield. For all new enquiries that you receive, you can quickly and politely request that they contact your recruitment provider to discuss becoming a PSL supplier, panellist or second-tier supplier.

That supplier can then genuinely vet their suitability for you, in the case of a Master Vendor agreement. If this is not the case, your single supplier can simply state that they aren't looking for additional agencies at present.

If you are the type of person who might conscientiously worry that you are throwing the proverbial hospital pass to your trusted suppler, then you needn't be. The reality is that a high percentage of enquiring recruiters will probably drop the hunt as soon as they hear that it is being governed by another recruiter, or even a competitor. It will naturally and significantly lessen the volume of enquiries that are received. If you're still worried, have the conversation with your recruiter and see how they feel about it. There is a good chance they will welcome the opportunity to chat with their competition, something that doesn't happen enough between recruiters.

Pulling it all together

By this stage, my hope is that we have together eroded many of the misunderstandings and false beliefs that make working with recruitment suppliers much more challenging than it needs to be. We've also covered a suite of structures and concepts, some of which will suit the nature of your business needs more than others.

On that note; if you're unsure where to start or are feeling overwhelmed about how to move forward from here, just trust in this. You now have a better knowledge of what recruiters need from you to be able to do a good job on your behalf. Give them the time and the information that empowers them to do a quality job on your behalf. Plus, expect more from them in return. The rest should follow. You'll remember the detail of the points in this book that interested you the most, as and when you need them. If you don't, just go over the contents page to prompt your memory.

The above said... If you haven't already done so, I would recommend these as your next steps:

1. Think about which recruiters you want to continue working with. Politely bring the other working relationships to an end.
2. Book an exploratory meeting with your favoured supplier or suppliers. If you don't have any, ask for referrals from similar businesses or look for examples online that have a healthy social endorsement or significant volumes of positive reviews.
3. In that meeting, tell your supplier(s) about any changes you plan to make or new approaches you're invested in

- whatever resonated with you the most from this book. The most important thing here is that they see and hear that you understand why more of a 'partnership' will work better, and that you plan to work more closely with them.
4. Ask what proposals they have or what they plan to do differently for you in return.

A favour to ask...

Thank you for reading this book. Hopefully you will be closer to achieving your business hiring goals as a result, and I will be one step closer to achieving my goal of positively influencing the reputation and quality of the recruitment industry as a whole.

If you found any of it to be of use, or felt that this information was unique in any way, I would be extremely thankful if you could review it on Amazon.

I sincerely wish you every success in building a mutually beneficial and successful partnership with your key suppliers. I hope it results in you getting what you need, and in a trouble-free, cost-effective way.

Thanks,

Simon

This book was written by Simon Berry, an experienced end-hirer, ex-recruiter, business consultant and Founder and CEO of Appoint Group, a highly regarded recruitment consultancy.